In the Morning

Debra Ronan

ISBN 978-1-63885-854-6 (Paperback)
ISBN 978-1-63885-863-8 (Digital)

Covenant Books
11661 Hwy 707
Murrells Inlet, SC 29576
www.covenantbooks.com

Photo Credits to Cheryl Jonelis
thank you for reminding me of the sunrise.

Day 1

Mar 18

🩶Good morning, my pink sisters! Please know that I prayed for you this morning. I pray that God will go before each and every one of you whether to a procedure, a doctor's appointment, or any other place that life brings you today. I pray that *He* make it a place of peace and safety.

🩶🩶🩶Dear Heavenly Father, I pray for every woman on this page. I pray that Your grace and love would wrap around them like a hug and that they would feel Your love. I pray, Lord, that as each one of us goes through this battle in our own way, we will remember that You are in control and that You asked that we cast all anxiety and fear on You because You love us so much that You are willing to take that from us so that we don't have to carry it. I thank You, Lord, for yet another day to be able to love, to be there for my family, and to make new friends. All glory and honor to You the healer and sustainer of my soul. Amen!

Isaiah 41:10—So do not fear, for I am with you; do not be dismayed, for I am your God. I will strengthen you and help you; I will uphold you with righteous right hand.

Day 2

Mar 19

💟 Good morning, my pink sisters, and yes, I did pray for you all this morning. And I will continue to pray for you every morning because what else can I do for you? I read this page, and I see the pain and the joy. I see the loneliness, and I see the strength. I draw my strength from God. He is who I run to in my time of need. And I understand that not everybody feels that way, but it's what I do. When I pray in the morning for you all, it's not just for the ones who are in agreement with me, but it's for all of you because I truly believe that God brings peace even in our most difficult times. I don't know a lot about different types of breast cancer, and I don't know a lot about different types of treatment, or what the right decision is. But what I do know is that if I bring my needs to God in prayer and petition and thankfulness, He will meet my needs one way or another.

💟 💟 💟 Dear Heavenly Father, I pray for all the women on this page today. I pray that they would see Your mighty hand, working in their life. And when we think that we're down and out, and when there's no more to be done, that's when You show up, and Your glory revealed. Lord, I know it's hard in these times to understand how much You love us when we're in so much pain, but You never give us more than we can handle. You use all that we go through for Your glory if we are willing to look. So I thank You today for going ahead of me and setting a place of peace where I don't have to be alone. And this is what I pray for all of these women. I pray that they would never feel alone, and they would always know that they can call on Your name at any time. Amen!

Day 3

Mar 20

Good morning, my pink sisters. I prayed for you today. I heard a solid word this morning. In 2 Timothy 4:16–18, Paul is facing the tribunal and has no support from his friends who have abandoned him. Although he may feel abandoned, he asked God to forgive those who have not supported him. I have read many stories and posts from women who are in this battle and feel abandoned. Their spouses, family, friends, and God have left them in their time of need. But I assure you, my sisters, that although humans fail, our *God* never fails. It is when our feelings of loneliness and abandonment consume us that we cannot feel His omnipresence. He never leaves us. Even when we choose the dark, He is there. When we are at our end, His mighty right hand lifts us high into His kingdom. Not even death can separate us from God. My sisters, if you are feeling alone, abandoned, and unloved, please know *God* loves you and is with you. I love you and think of you all often. Forgive those who do not support you and allow *God* into your presence where you can rest.

💟 💟 2 Timothy 4:16–18—At my first defense, no one came to my support, but everyone deserted me. May it not be held against them. But the Lord stood at my side and gave me strength, so that through me the message might be fully proclaimed and all the Gentiles might hear it. And I was delivered from the lion's mouth. The Lord will rescue me from every evil attack and will bring me safely to His heavenly kingdom. To him be the glory forever and ever. Amen.

💟 💟 💟 Dear Heavenly Father, in our time of need, when we feel abandoned and alone, help us remember You are there. When the darkness comes to us, and we cannot see, shine your light. Let us know You are there. When our loved ones and friends fail us, help us to forgive. Let us know You are there. And when we lift Your name in glory and cry out in prayer, let us know You are there. Amen!

💟 If no one has told you today that you are loved, I love you. 💟

Day 4

Mar 20

💟 Good morning, my pink sisters. Today is going to be a good day. Yesterday, I got a call from my boss, informing me I was directly exposed to COVID through a coworker. And for a moment there, I got scared because, for the last few months, it's been one thing after the other. I thought to myself, *How the heck am I going to deal with COVID?* So after I had my moment, which does happen, I reminded myself that God is in control. That if He leads me to it, He will bring me through it. So this morning as I just finished my Bible reading, I watched one of my favorite pastors do a sermon (Charles Stanley). He reminded me of this.

💟 💟 Philippians 4:7
And the peace of God, which transcends all understanding will guard your heart and your mind in Christ Jesus.

This reminds me not to be anxious for nothing if bad news comes because I have God's peace, which although I don't understand, I know He is faithful to give.

💗 💗 💗 Dear Heavenly Father, please be with each one of my pink sisters today as we battle those moments of bad news and good news. I will remember that Your peace is always with us. Although at times we may waiver for a short time, bring us back, Lord, always to that peace that transcends all understanding. Guard our hearts and our minds, Lord, and that be always with us. We are never alone. God bless all of you today!

Day 5

Mar 23

🩶 Good morning, my pink sisters! I prayed for you this morning. I prayed that God would be with all of you today and that no matter what you're going through, His peace would be abundant and that you would know that you are not alone. I know a lot of us are going into surgery and treatment today, and I pray for you, and I pray for peace over you. I pray for peace for your loved ones. I pray for peace for your doctors and any staff with who you would come in contact. If nobody's told you today that they love you, I love you, and God loves you.

🩶 🩶 🩶 Dear Heavenly Father, be with these courageous, strong, beautiful women today. Everything that You will has a reason, Lord. We may not always know that reason, and in the thick of the fire, Lord, there are so many emotions to deal with. But in all this, Lord, I ask that You help us to stand with our feet firmly on the solid rock and that we would be able to see You in our lives moving. That we would be able to feel your peace, and no we are not alone, knowing that You walk beside us, guiding us, in front of us, making a way. Lord, don't ever let us walk ahead of You on our own, in our own strength. I thank You for this day, Lord, and I thank You for these women; and I ask that You would bless them. Amen!

Day 6

Mar 24

💕 Good morning, my pink sisters. I've been praying for you this morning and thinking about you. My post is usually done really early, but I took the day off from work today and stayed in bed until eight-thirty. I'm usually up between four and four-thirty, so that was a treat for me. Sometimes you just got to take care of yourself when you can.

💕 But I didn't forget about you, ladies! Dear Heavenly Father, in the name of Jesus, I pray for these women who fight a battle every day. I pray that You, Lord, would be their strength, the solid rock on which they stand. And Your peace that surpasses all worldly understanding would be given to them. Be with their loved ones and the caretakers, Lord. Give them strength and hope. Help them, Lord, to love these women in the way that they needed to be loved. And when they cannot feel that love, Lord, I ask that You would remind them to turn their hearts toward You. We are never alone when we have You, Lord, my Father, my God. Amen!

BE BLESSED TODAY! AND IF NO ONE HAS TOLD YOU THEY LOVE YOU, I LOVE YOU, AND GOD LOVES YOU! 💕 💕 💕 💕 💕 💕 💕

Day 7

Mar 26

Good morning, my pink sisters, I am praying for you this morning, and I will be praying for you throughout the day. The scripture I read this morning talked about trust and confidence in the Lord. It took me a really long time to get to the trust part, and now I'm there and working on the confidence to allow Him to work in my life and to stand by His word knowing that He'll take care of me every step of the way. I was going through the post, and I noticed that there's a lot of our pink sisters out there who have people in their lives who are toxic. And it makes me sad. I've been in a place before where my husband totally hurt me. My husband is not a bad person. He's just human, and I can't put too much faith in another human to take care of me. My faith has to be in God. He is the provider of everything. And there's nothing that goes on in my life that I cannot bring to God and ask for good orderly direction. I know some situations are much worse than others, and I wish that I had some way of getting all of us out of our battles painless, but I do have this: Go to God and pray for yourself and for the people around you. He is listening and wants you to come to Him with your whole heart.

💟 💟 Jeremiah 17:7

But blessed is the one who trusts in the Lord, whose confidence is in Him.

💟 💟 💟 Dear Heavenly Father, I ask, Lord, that You would be with each and every woman in this group. I ask that they may learn to trust in You, Lord, and have confidence in Your ability to take care of them every day. There is not one need that we have that You cannot fill. There is not one situation in our lives that You cannot help us overcome. I pray for these women who may have spouses or partners in their life who are just not stepping up emotionally, Lord, and I ask that You would help these women to feel loved and to know that You care about them right down to the smallest detail. Be with these beautiful women today, Lord. In these battles, give each and every one of them the strength to make it through today. Help them to find the willingness to come to You in prayer and ask for what they need. For You are the provider, the Father, and lover of our souls. Amen!

Day 8

Mar 29

Good morning, my pink sisters. I prayed for you this morning. I hope you all had a blessed weekend. I did a little self-care and cleaned my house, went out Saturday, and got some fresh air. Then I went to church on Sunday, hanging out being lazy, LOL. Honestly this morning, I'm having a really hard time sharing with you all. I was reading some of the posts over the weekend along with the comments. It seemed as though a lot of the women on this page don't want to hear about God. And I completely understand, especially if you don't have a relationship with Him, or you don't believe, or maybe you've had a bad experience. Turning to God, is what I know, it's who I am. And I know that His grace is sufficient. He never once promised that my life would be easy. As a matter of fact, He said that if I follow Him, it'll probably be harder. So I was a little discouraged to share because I never want to offend other people, but I cannot turn my back on God, especially because He's done so much for me. So I've decided that I will continue to pray and share His word with you all. I believe that's what He wants me to do through this experience of breast cancer. I love that my prayers for you to God bring you peace and comfort.

2 Corinthians 12:9—But He said to me, "My grace is sufficient for you, for my power is made perfect in weakness." Therefore I will boast all the more gladly about my weaknesses, so that Christ's power may rest on me.

Dear Heavenly Father, I'm not sure anything I've faced in life has made me feel weaker than finding out I had cancer. But, Lord, in my weakness, You make me strong. You show me how to lean on you, and through Your grace and love for me, You bought me here. I pray for these women, Lord, for those who know You and don't know You, that your love and mercy would protect and guide them. I know, Lord, that it is hard for some people to understand Your love for them, especially when they're going through something like this. Bring peace, Lord. Bring open hearts and open minds that You might be able to show Yourself to those who are hurting. And for those sisters who believe in You, I asked for continued strength and faith. Lord, sometimes, it is very hard to have faith, but I know Your grace is sufficient for me. Be with us today, Father God. Go before us and all that is ahead of us and set a place of peace for us. Be with every surgeon and medical team who takes care of the women in the support group. Amen!

Day 9

Mar 30

🩶 Good morning, my pink sisters. I prayed for you this morning. And I was thinking about how difficult this journey is. I know God is with me every step of the way, but I am also a human who worries. I sometimes am so overwhelmed with news, and I don't turn to God first. And this is what I'm working on—to immediately go to the Father. I know that He already knows what is going to happen in my life, so nothing that I tell Him is going to be a surprise. I also know that everything *He* does is for my good, whether I agree with Him or not. I strive to be the kind of woman who immediately turns to the Father and knows she is safe. So pray for me about that. If I can do that, then everything else will be okay.

🩶 🩶 Psalm 112:7—They will have no fear of bad news; their hearts are steadfast, trusting in the Lord.

🩶 🩶 🩶 Dear Heavenly Father, I thank You, Lord, for all that You do for me and all the women in this group. I ask, Lord, that today You will help us to not fear any bad news but to look forward to all the good news You have to give us. Make our heart steadfast, Lord, trusting in You, Lord Father, that in all of this, You are in every single moment. Lord, help me and the women in this group who sometimes find ourselves going straight into panic mode or anxious thoughts, but we would turn our hearts and minds toward You, knowing that You hold us in Your mighty right hand. Amen!

Day 10

Mar 31

Good morning, my pink sisters. I prayed for you this morning and asked God to show up wherever you are and reveal Himself to you. In your homes, waiting rooms, operating room, wherever you may be today, remember He is there. I am reminded this week that Jesus was also in a place He did not want to be. He went to the Father to ask that He may pass by this moment but only if it be His will. Knowing there was going to be a place of suffering and sorrow, Jesus obeyed and was brought to the cross. *But* in the end, *glory* awaited Him. He did the Father's will, and the Father was faithful.

Luke 22:42—Father, if it be Your will, take this cup from me; yet not my will, but Yours be done.

Dear Heavenly Father, be with us today as we willfully obey You. Even when it is scary, we know we will endure sorrow and pain. We ask, Lord, that if this cup cannot pass us, You would give us the strength to endure. Jesus died on the cross so we could be set free, not only of sin but also of anxiety and fear of sickness and death. You, Lord God, are the lover of our souls. You bring peace and renew happiness. For all that is taken shall be restored. Amen!

Day 11

April 1

🩶 Good morning, my pink sisters. I'm praying for you this morning. I'm praying that God's peace will be with you and that through this trial, our faith will grow. I started a new devotional today. It's called *Hidden Potential: Revealing What God Can Do Through You*. I might say my first reading was awesome. Here is the question that stuck out in my mind the most. What if God's plan isn't to fix the things that have fractured my faith but instead to show His power through them, making my faith stronger than ever? What would that mean for me?

🩶 🩶 Romans 8:28—And we know that in all things God works for the good of those who love Him, who have been called according to His purpose.

🩶 🩶 🩶 Dear Heavenly Father, I pray that You would be with us today. Lord, what if Your plan is not to fix the things that have fractured our faith? But to show Your power more than ever and stronger than ever in our lives. I know You have a plan for me, Lord, as you do for every woman in this group. Your plans are always to prosper us and never to hurt us, always to bring us closer to Your love. Be with us, Lord, as You reveal Your plans for us. That in obedience, we would follow You even if we think we are not qualified. For the women who are struggling to turn to You, Lord, may you gently turn their eyes toward home and renew their faith. Amen!

Day 12

April 3

💗 Good morning, my *pink* sisters. I prayed for you this morning, and God is with us. May your hearts and souls be refreshed and encouraged as you reach out to Him.

💗 💗 Romans 15:5–6
May the God who gives endurance and encouragement give you the same attitude of mind toward each other that Christ Jesus had, so that with one mind and voice you may glorify the God and Father of our Lord Jesus Christ.

💗 💗 💗 Dear Heavenly Father, help us, Lord, as Your believers, to encourage those around us. We have You in our lives, Lord, and we want to share You with those who do not know You. Even in our own times of darkness, let us remember we have a light. The light should not be hidden but used as a beacon to guide people to You. Be with my pink sisters today. Give them strength, guidance, encouragement, and rest. Send your light to shine on those lost in darkness. Believers and unbelievers both, free us from our fear. Remind us of Your victory over sin and death. Help us, Lord, to be thankful for what You have provided. Amen!

HE HAS RISEN! I'm feeling happy.

Day 13

April 5

💗 Good morning, my pink sisters. I prayed for you this morning. My reading this morning talked about "perfect love expels all fear." The perfect love of God covers all my fears. I have fear sometimes. Sometimes I'm in it for a bit before I turn it over. Thank God I'm a work in progress, LOL. The reading also talked about how, "We are not perfect, and on this side of heaven, we cannot love perfectly." This made me think about my expectations of others and how I sometimes expect others to fill my cup. True, pure, unfailing love can only come from God. He is love, and His love is perfect. Have a blessed day.

💗 💗 Psalm 56:3—When I am afraid, I will put my trust in You.

💗 💗 💗 Dear Heavenly Father, I thank You, God, for Your perfect love that casts out all fears. You are there waiting and willing to show me Your perfect and endless love. Be with me and all the ladies in this group. Remind us, God, that You and only You can love us perfectly. Help us to not put the expectation on others to fill a place in us that only You can fill. Be with those headed to surgery, doctor's appointments, and all other places to be in peace, knowing we have You God, and You have us. I love You, God, and I am thankful for all You have done for me. Amen!

2 Corinthians 12:9— But He said to me,"My grace is sufficient for you, for my power is made perfect in weakness" Therefore I will boast all the more gladly about my weaknesses, so that Christ's power may rest on me.

Day 14

April 6

Good morning, my pink sisters. I prayed for you this morning. I am having a bit of a morning. I prayed this morning, but my words seem to fall short. I have a lot of things going on as I'm sure you can all relate. My human emotions are getting the best of me. I feel like because my BC has been kind of moving right along for lack of a better phrase. Everybody thinks I'm back 100 percent. Nobody stops to think that I'm tired, sometimes emotionally drained, and needing rest and comfort myself. Well, then I turn to God in prayer, and not really knowing what to say, I pray. But I feel like my heart hasn't let everything out. God in His usual manner brings me to Romans 8:26. I then realized, God always knows my heart and has a resting place for me. Because the world does not meet my needs, it is Him I rely on.

💟 💟 Romans 8:26—In the same way, the Spirit helps us in our weakness. We do not know what we ought to pray for, but the Spirit himself intercedes for us through wordless groans.

💟 💟 💟 Dear Heavenly Father, thank You, God, for knowing me so well. Thank You for the Holy Spirit who goes to You on my behalf. God, be with us today as we seek shelter from this world. A world that cannot possibly meet our needs. A world that cannot refresh me as You refresh me. In all we do, Father God, let it be for You. Be with us, comfort us, and fill us. Amen!

Day 15

April 7

Good morning, my pink sisters. I prayed for you this morning. Getting a late start. My husband and I hopped on a plane yesterday and went to our house in Florida. We were coming for spring break next week but left early. This was in my reading today, and boy it got me thinking. *After this, will I keep my face toward God; or having received my blessing and mercy, will I go back to the way it was?* I will never be able to be who I was, and I'm okay with that. God has renewed a new path for me. You, ladies, are a huge part of it. I never thought I would be praying and sharing daily on a BC support group page, and yet God has led me to you, and I am thankful. Let us never go back to a time God was not first in our lives. Let us never forgot how much He did for us even in this season.

Isaiah 43:19—See, I am doing a new thing! Now it springs up; do you not perceive it? I am making a way in the wilderness and streams in the wasteland.

Dear Heavenly Father, let us never forget Your grace and mercy. How easy it is when things get better to turn away and slip back into old valleys. Lord, mercy is new every day, and I thank You for it. Make a new way and a new stream for us as we are in the wilderness. Bring us out, Lord, and set our feet on a straight path, which leads to You. I thank You for these women, Lord, that You care about us, and we care about one another. May You be with each and every one of us as we call upon Your mighty name. Amen!

Day 16

April 8

Good morning, my pink sisters. I prayed for you this morning. I was listening to a sermon by Charles Stanley, one of my favorites, titled "Living Life to the Fullest." It reminded me of all those who came before me who may have thought, *What the heck is God doing?* I've been there before. I'm sure many of you have been in the desert somewhere else in life, and BC is just another speed bump. I have been over many speed bumps in life, but the *C* word was what really stopped me in my tracks. I don't know why, maybe because the thought of going home was scarier than I thought. In Hebrews 12, it talks about running the race well, *have I?* I am not the first Christian to suffer in life, and many more before me suffered worse. Jesus suffered for me more than I will ever suffer for Him. My hope is to run the race set before me, speed bumps and all, in a manner that glorifies God and serves others.

Hebrews 12:1–3—Therefore, since we are surrounded by such a great cloud of witnesses, let us throw off everything that hinders and the sin that so easily entangles. And let us run with perseverance the race marked out for us, fixing our eyes on Jesus, the pioneer and perfecter of faith. For the joy set before Him He endured the cross, scorning it's shame, and sat down at the right hand of the throne of God. Consider Him who endured such opposition from sinners, so that you will not grow weary and lose heart.

Dear Heavenly Father, may we run well the race You have put us on, always remembering You are with us. Even when there are speed bumps, Lord, help us to know You are there. I want to run my race and serve others so Your name is glorified. Father, be with my sisters and make known to them Your love and Your promises. You promise You would never leave us or forsake us. You would always be with us. For my sisters who feel they are in this race alone, *you are not*! The author of life who wrote us into existence is with you. Lord, let us see You today. Amen!

Day 17

April 11

💟 Good morning, my pink sisters, I prayed for you this morning. I have a week before radiation starts. Nineteen rounds and then tamoxifen for five years. I'm so thankful that God is my refuge. He allows me to be covered and safe if that's where I choose to be, or I can be frantic and worried not relying on His promise of a safe place. Sometimes I worry, and it may take me a bit to get my mind back on God. This week, as we rest and prepare for what comes next, as we seek Him in prayer and meditation, may we find His place of refuge that God has for us.

💟 💟 Psalm 62:5–8—Find rest, O my soul, in God alone; my hope comes from Him. He alone is my rock and my salvation; He is my fortress, I will not be shaken. My salvation and my honor depend on God; He is my mighty rock, my refuge.

💟 💟 💟 Dear Heavenly Father, thank You, God, for being our rock and our salvation. May we never be shaken from knowing You are always with us, in control of what happens. I pray, God, in my times of need, I remember You comfort me and cover me. God, may we feel the promise You made to never leave us or forsake us. Amen!

Numbers 6:24–26—"The Lord bless you and keep you; the Lord make his face shine on you and be gracious to you; the Lord turn his face toward you and give you peace."

Day 18

April 12

Good morning, my pink sisters. I prayed for you this morning. I was listening to a sermon, from Charles Stanley, "Grace in Times of Trial." In 2 Corinthians 12, Paul talks about the thorn in his side, and how he has asked God to remove it. God's reply was, "My grace is sufficient." This is not the first time I've read this and thought, *I'm going to have trials and sickness and other things that I will pray about, and God will say, "Yes, no, or not now."* Therefore, His grace becomes sufficient for me. As I was praying about that, God put Psalm 69 on my heart—a psalm I have not read.

In the beginning, David is crying out to the Lord, overwhelmed with his circumstances. As I read the beginning of this psalm, it truly describes how I felt when the doctor called to say, "You have cancer." Cancer is a physical, emotional, and spiritual enemy; but as I cried out to God, He answered. In 2 Corinthians 12:9, "But He said to me, 'My grace is sufficient for you, for My power is made perfect in weakness.'" Therefore, I will boast all the more gladly about my weaknesses so that Christ's power may rest on me.

Psalm 69:1–3—Save me, O God for the waters have come up to my neck. I sink in the miry depths, where there is no foothold. I have come into the deep waters; the floods engulf me. I am worn out calling for help; my throat is parched. My eyes fail, looking for my God.

Dear Heavenly Father, "You have cancer" is something none of us wanted to hear. Father, I cried out to You to let this cup pass if it is Your will. Lord, we come to You with many requests, most times that we or others will not suffer. But, Lord, if we do not suffer, how do we learn of Your grace? Help us, Lord, in the suffering. Remind us You are with us in the suffering and that good things come from our trials. We give You praise and glory, Father God, for, in our weakness, You are strong! I thank You for every woman on this page. I lift them to You, Father, whether Your answer is yes, no, or not now. May we accept the outcome, for You know our path and would never lead us astray. Amen!

Day 19

April 13

Good morning, my pink sisters. I prayed for you today. How often I start my day in prayer, asking God to heal this and fix that, thanking Him, of course. But sometimes, I'm so wrapped in myself I forget *He* is *God* and is worthy of all my worship and praise not just my list of needs. So today I am focusing on giving God all my worship, for how awesome and mighty He is. He knows my heart, so He knows my needs. He is a great *God,* the *I Am*.

Psalm 104:1—Praise the Lord, my soul. Lord my God, you are very great; you are clothed with splendor and majesty.

Dear Heavenly Father, how excellent Your name is! How vast and how wide is Your awesomeness! We praise You, Father, for all the beauty You have created. For how You love us even when we are not lovely. Father, I pray that today, even in our suffering, we will choose to worship You. For You are good, and great is Your faithfulness. Amen!

Psalm 23:1–2—The Lord is my Shepard, I lack nothing.
He makes me lie down in green pastures; he leads me
beside quiet waters

Day 20

April 14

💗 Good morning, my pink sisters. I prayed for you this morning, thinking of God's grace and how He loves us where we are at, before, and after accepting Him. Some think you have to clean up before God will accept you. Believe me, that isn't the case. God came to me at my lowest point. I was in a sin that I thought would end me, but instead, He took that sin and saved me. I am learning, sometimes the hard way, that God doesn't expect perfection, just willingness to change. He will sometimes press us forward so we will grow closer to Him. When we rebel toward God, even when it is clear what He wants, He redirects our path. This is what BC has done for me. I've been running from God for a long time, not willing to step out in faith, and now I am drawing closer to him. Whatever happens, God knows, beginning, middle, and end. It is well with my soul. 💗

Philippians 3:14—I press on toward the goal to win the prize for which God has called me heavenward in Christ Jesus.

Dear Heavenly Father, thank You, thank You, thank You for Your grace. For loving us even when we were in our sin. Willing to take us as-is and transform us to who You destined us to be. I am in awe of Your goodness. Help us today, Father, to press forward to the goal, which is eternity with you. And may we endure our path as we go from beginning to the end, knowing You are in every step, situation, doctor's appointment, and treatment every dark moment where we cry out, "Abba Father, be with me!" Change us from broken vessels to carriers of the light. Amen!

Isaiah 43:2—When you pass through the waters, I will be with you; and when you pass through the rivers, they will not sweep over you. When you walk through the fire, you will not be burned; the flames will not set you ablaze.

Day 21

April 16

Good morning, my pink sisters. I prayed for you today. I'm just getting ready to head home from my vacation. I'll be starting radiation on Monday. One good thing is that my son who is in the Navy will be coming home and spending the first two weeks with me. God is so good. Don't get me wrong. The devil is coming at me left and right; but my God is greater, my God is stronger, and He will never leave me.

Isaiah 25:1—O LORD, You are my God; I will exalt You and praise Your name, for in perfect faithfulness You have done marvelous things, things planned long ago.

Dear Heavenly Father, thank You, Lord, for this day. Be with all of us on this journey as we go forward. I thank You, Lord, for the rest You have provided me and my time alone with You. You have a plan, and it is all for my good. Amen!

Day 22

April 18

Good morning, my pink sisters. I prayed for you this morning. Do you ever have those moments when you say something and then immediately wish you could take it back? You're hurt and discouraged. You feel like you need to defend yourself and all that you're going through, and the words just come pouring out of your mouth. Well, I've had a couple of those moments. The problem is that no matter what I'm going through and what my trial is, I'm still responsible for what I say. And I need to remember that I have Christ in me, so no matter what my trial is, my words should always be kind and never condemning. And it is so, so hard when you're suffering, and people just aren't getting it, and you want a kind word yourself. But remember, Jesus never spoke harshly even to those who hurt Him. May I be like Jesus today.

Proverbs 16:24—Gracious words are a honeycomb, sweet to the soul and healing to the bones.

Dear Heavenly Father, be with us today, Lord, in our trials. Help us, Lord, to be aware of the words that we speak toward others even if their words toward us are hurtful. Your Words are like sweet honey, Lord, that can heal our soul and bring strength to our bones, Lord. Lord, help me today to be mindful of my thoughts, my words, and my actions. Those who are looking for the light will see us today in the word, and I ask that we would shine brightly for You and be an example, not only in action but also in word. How sweet and loving You are. Amen!

Day 23

April 19

Good morning, my pink sisters, I prayed for you today. I go today to have my trial run for my radiation. I feel good this morning. I have a very busy day, and my son is coming in from the Navy for the next two weeks. I'm totally excited about that. But what I'm really excited about is obeying God. You all have heard me talk about my bookmarkers, totally designed by God. And although I've mailed out quite a few of these bookmarkers to some of you women, God put this upon my heart with the plan to hand them out at treatment. God's plan is always so intertwined with answering prayers for us. My son, who will be coming with me to radiation, is not a believer. And I have been praying for him for years, and God has orchestrated it so that He will watch me minister to others. I can tell you if you don't know what a mighty God we serve. And everything that He does for us—good, bad, or indifferent—is always for our good. Seek His good today, pray for the revealing of His purpose, and most importantly obey. Obey the Word God has given you even when it doesn't look the way we want it to look because He always has our best lives in mind.

Philippians 4:13—I can do all things through Christ who strengthens me.

Dear Heavenly Father, be with us today as we obey Your Word. Help us, Lord, in all situations to follow You. Lord, today I head out to start my treatment. I ask that You would be with me, that Your piece would go before me, and that I will have nothing to fear. I asked that all that I encounter today would be led by You. I will spread Your love, Lord, to all those I encounter today. Thank You for this day, God, and everything that it brings. I can do all things through You as long as I obey. Amen!

Day 24

April 21

💗 Good morning, my pink sisters. I prayed for you this morning that you would have *God* moments today. Those things that happen are only from *God*, and we know it. For example, at my appointment yesterday, I was wondering how I could give out the bookmarkers when you're in and out? How was my son going to witness God at work? Well, I came out of radiation. The room was full, and there was my son chatting with the lady next to him. She was a Christian, talking to him about Jesus. That's how our *God* works. She got bookmarkers, and we chatted a minute. *God* is so awesome.

💗 💗 Joshua 1:9—Have I not commanded you? Be strong and courageous. Do not be afraid; do not be discouraged, for the Lord your God will be with you wherever you go.

💗 💗 💗 Dear Heavenly Father, help me to always remember to not be afraid or discouraged due to circumstances. To always look for the *God* moments that You show every day. Thank You, *God*, for that moment yesterday and for putting in me the excitement to see more. Be with my sisters in pink, *God*. Show up wherever they are and remind them how You love them. Amen!

Day 25

April 22

Good morning, my pink sisters. I prayed for you this morning. Thank you to everyone who was praying for me last night. God has brought a new day and a new word to think on. In our obedience, we cry out to God to save us from our fears. In His perfect love, He shows up. How many times must He show me? He parted the Red Sea, the fires of wrath, and the three men in the furnace delivered, unharmed by the flame. Who delivered His people out of Egypt? Our mighty God who gives to us all we need and who sent His only Son to die so we could live. How many times will I fear although I know He is with me and will keep me safe?

Isaiah 43:2–3—When you pass through the waters, I will be with you; and when you pass through the rivers, they will not sweep over you. When you walk through the fire, you will not be burned, the flames will not set you ablaze, for I am the Lord, your God, the holy one of Israel, your savior.

Heavenly Father, forgive my untrusting heart. Forgive my weakness. I know, Lord, You are with me, and not one hair on my head should be amiss. Father, fill me with courage for another day and expectation of Your greatness. Thank You for walking me through the water, past the raging river, and out of the flames. Amen!

Day 26

April 23

💗 Good afternoon, my pink sisters. I prayed for you today. God's covenant through the death of Jesus on the cross is about grace. *Praise God*, I think to myself as I listen to the sermon. I started to think, *If it were the Old Testament times, I would be in trouble*.

I grew up breaking rules and never learning lessons (so I thought). I never knew about grace. I figured I'm bad. I don't like myself, and no one else likes me. What a relief when I found Jesus and learned God would take me cracks and all because of this covenant. It's my progress, not my perfection, He seeks. In my brokenness, it's His beauty that drives me to Him; and in His death, He receives me with His arms open. May you find this is grace in Him today.

💗 💗 Luke 22:19—And He who took bread gave thanks and broke it, and gave it to them, "This is my body given for you; do this in remembrance of me."

💗 💗 💗 Dear Heavenly Father, I pray, Lord, and lift my sisters to You with our brokenness and all. May we see in our brokenness what You saw in dying on the cross for each and every one of us. Today, I ask, Lord, You would give grace in abundance; and as we seek You, we would find You with arms open wide and with love and grace for us. Amen!

Day 27

April 24

💗 Good morning, pink sisters. I prayed for you this morning and will continue to pray. I was reading Psalm 119. Many verses talk of suffering and how we should delight in it. If we know God's Word, we know He draws us to Him in our suffering. He is our comfort and refuge. I am so thankful for the knowledge of God's Word. I could not imagine my suffering alone without God.

💗 💗 Psalm 119:50—My comfort in my suffering is this: Your promise preserves my life.

💗 💗 💗 Dear Heavenly Father, thank You, Lord, that in my suffering, Your promises remain true. I am drawn to You, and the Holy Spirit keeps me close. May I never forget Your Word. May it always be kept in my heart. Amen!

Day 28

April 26

Good morning, my pink sisters! I prayed for you this morning and have a prayer request. Radiation is still on hold due to difficulty with the software. I spoke with my doctor last night and was struggling with whether I wanted to do radiation or not. It's preventative for me, and I'm praying. Please pray for clarity in what God wants and for me to make the right decision.

I often wonder about God's plan for me. Where will He take me and use me for His purpose? So when I read Jeremiah 29:11, and He says, "plans to prosper you and not to harm you," I had to think it through. How is He, in this season of BC, prospering me? How is He keeping me from harm? We lose a lot in BC—our breast or part of, our hair, our health, our family, our friends, and, sometimes, life itself.

What I realized is that my prosperity has come in my relationship with God. With BC, He has shown me how to truly rely on and draw close to Him. This body is temporary, but life with God is forever. One day, we will all pass from this world and step into eternity, and our relationship with Jesus matters. We will one day be free of sickness, and we will be in our new bodies. He also promises in Jeremiah 29:11 "hope and a future." I have hope; therefore, I have a future, not only on this earth and in this body but also in God's kingdom with Him, free of sickness in His glorious presence.

Jeremiah 29:11—"For I know the plans I have for you," declares the Lord, "plans to prosper you and not to harm you, plans to give you hope and a future."

Dear Heavenly Father, thank You, God, for Your plans. I realize Your will is perfect. Help us, Lord, to always remember that Your path is straight, and Your promises are true. You never said it would be easy. You did say if I follow you, I would have trials; and through them, You would be with me. Give us strength for our trials so we might run our race well and find prosperity in Your grace and mercy. Amen!

Day 29

April 27

💗 Good morning, my pink sisters. I prayed for you this morning. I'm off with my boys today. I'm going to start radiation again tomorrow. Yes, I've decided to go. At the beginning of my BC, God laid the bookmarkers on my heart. He wants me to give them to people at my treatment. If I don't go, I can't pass them out. I'm learning to obey even when I don't want to. Satan gave me a minute there to get off track. He is cunning and will use our minds against us if we don't stay strong. Be strong, my sisters. God has a plan for you.

💗 💗 Numbers 6:24–26—The Lord bless you and keep you; the Lord make His face shine on you and be gracious to you; the Lord turn His face toward you and give you peace.

💗 💗 💗 Dear Heavenly Father, thank You, Lord, for Your path. Your path leads to home. Thank You for Your grace and mercy toward us. May we find comfort in You today as we obey even when it's uncomfortable, and we want to run. Give us strength in difficulty and courage to do Your will. Amen!

Psalm 34:18—The Lord is close to the brokenhearted and saves those who are crushed in spirit.

Day 30

April 29

Good morning, my pink sisters. I prayed for you this morning. There was a time when although I believed, I did not follow God's Word. I ran from God most of my life. I was afraid. I didn't think I was good enough for Him. I could believe in Him all I wanted, but His blessings were not for this wretch. About two years ago, I turned a spiritual corner. I'm not even sure how. In God's timing, I heard him knocking and decided to open the door for Him. After reading Revelation 3:20, I see that even as believers, God knocks when we close the door on Him. He asked us to open up to Him once again so we might eat together. If you have shut the door on God and feel you cannot return, open the door. He is waiting for you. God loves you unconditionally. Even now in your brokenness, He is knocking. Receive Him, eat with Him, and allow Him to once again refresh your soul.

Revelation 3:20—Here I am! I stand at the door and knock. If anyone hears my voice and opens the door, I will come in and eat with him, and he with me.

💝 💝 💝 Dear Heavenly Father, please be with my sisters today. Whether they are believers who have shut the door, or maybe You're hearing the knock for the first time. Give them the strength to open the door. God, we are in a place of need in need of love, understanding, healing, good doctors, and treatments, but most of all, a need for You. Fill us, Lord, with the desire to return to You. As you urged the people of the churches and once again revealed to them that they need to turn back to You, allow us, Lord, father to return to You, to be made whole, and to fulfill Your purpose. Amen!

Day 31

May 5

💟 Good morning, my pink sisters. I prayed for you this morning. After reading my morning verse, I thought to myself, *The dark days are coming, but we who believe have hope*. I pray for those I love to call upon God and be saved. When I think about God's plan and cancer, I know He is using it for His good in order to minister to those who do not believe and to give witness to God's love, mercy, and grace. When people ask me about my *hope*, I give glory to God. For believers, for myself, I know there is a time when days will be darker than even now. *But* be of *hope*! Our salvation rests in God and in the *hope* of His return. Our message to those who have not called upon the one who saves will show in how we handle our trials. May we be the messengers of *hope* to those in the wilderness.

💟 💟 Romans 10:13—For, everyone who calls on the name of the Lord will be saved.

Dear Heavenly Father, thank You, Lord, for salvation. You have made it clear that the way to the Father is through the Son. We need only to call upon His name and be saved. Thank You, Lord, for every opportunity for us to share your message. Lord, for our family and friends who have yet to call upon you, I ask, Father, let us be a witness to who you are, even in trials. Never did You say the road was easy, but You did promise to be with us. Let us use this time to be a reflection of You to a world that is hurting. Amen!

Day 32

May 6

Good morning, my pink sisters, I prayed for you this morning. When I pray, sometimes I forget to take the time to watch God at work and then thank Him. Usually not with big things but the small things. Sometimes I pray for the same things every day, for example, my family's salvation. In Luke chapter 18, Jesus tells a parable about a widow who was relentless with her request for justice. Finally, the judge got tired of hearing her plea and granted justice to her. Jesus goes on to say, "Will God not do the same for those He loves?" God is just and faithful if we are faithful to pray in accordance with His will. Are we faithful with the big and small prayers? Do we watch for God to move even if we think He is taking too long? Do we thank Him even if the answer is no because we know He knows what's best? I'll be thinking about this today and asking God to help me be watchful and thankful.

Colossians 4:2—Devote yourself to prayer, being watchful and thankful.

💗 💗 💗 Dear Heavenly Father, thank You for Your justice in answered prayer. When we pray, Lord, may we come to You and then be watchful for Your answer and thankful for Your grace. Lord, be with us today and hear our prayers. Answer our pleas, Lord. May we never forget Your justice is love. Lord, give us acceptance of Your answer. For You are God and know what is best for us even if we don't agree. For all is to Your glory and kingdom. Amen!

Day 33

May 7

💟 Good morning, my pink sisters. I prayed for you this morning. I will seek you, God. My soul thirst for you. My body is weary where your water is not found. Lord, may You hear me and protect me. Help me to listen and know I am safe. May my children find refuge in Your name. You are the *I Am*, the strong tower. May Your name be praised forever. You are the rock on which I stand and where I find refuge from the storm. You, Lord, delivered me from my enemies, shielded me, and protected me. My trust is in you, Father. You are my hiding place when I cannot stand. You put my feet on steady ground, and I am safe.

💟 💟 Proverbs 18:10—The name of the Lord is a strong tower; the righteous run to it and are safe.

💟 💟 💟 Dear Heavenly Father, You are my rock, the one I hold onto in my time of need. Lord, thank You for allowing me into Your safe and protected dwelling place. Lift me, Lord, out of this pit and set my feet on the rock. You, God, are my shield, my defense against all enemies. In You, I put my trust. Be with me today, Lord. Be with us. As we seek refuge, Lord, from this weary place, may we find peace, and may we drink from Your water of life and be renewed. Amen!

Day 34

May 8

Good morning, my pink sisters. I prayed for you this morning. Well, my son left today after his three-week visit. Needless to say, this mom is very sad today. Being that he's in the Navy, I don't get to see him that often; and every time he leaves, it's just as hard as when he first left six years ago. But we had a lovely visit. He went to radiation with me, he hung out with me, he cared for me, and we just got to spend some really good time together. Now that I'm halfway through my radiation, I'm feeling a bit fatigued, and my skin is starting to feel like I have sunburn, and yet I'm trying to fix my eyes upon the Lord. He has walked everywhere that I have walked, He has felt everything that I am feeling, and He knows what my needs are so I trust in Him. He sits at the right hand of the Father and will never leave me or forsake me. I am praying that I can keep my eyes on the prize that I might run this race and run it well that all glory be given to God.

Hebrews 12:2—Let us fix our eyes on Jesus, the author and perfector of our faith, who for the joy set before him endured the cross, scorning its shame, and sat down at the right hand of the throne of God.

Dear Heavenly Father, thank You, Lord, for going before me. May I keep my eyes fixed on You and know that in the end, You will be waiting for me. Lord, may I look to You today and remember that You gave all so that I might have a race to run. Help me, Lord, to remember Your sacrifice for me, a sinner. Amen!

Day 35

May 11

Good morning, my pink sisters, I prayed for you today. Rejoice in suffering? hmm, okay, why would I do that? God says when we do, it brings perseverance, perseverance, character, and character, hope. I've been through suffering, and I have not looked for help but for the reason of my suffering. Why, God? Why am I going through this? Why me? What about my children? What about my family? When I read this today, and it's not the first time I've read this, God revealed to me that when I persevere through my suffering, it gives Him a chance to build my character; and then in the building of my character, He gives me hope and pours out His love into me through the Holy Spirit. I don't know what God's road has for me. I know it's had a lot of potholes and speed bumps. I know that there have been many times it's just like, really, God? And every time I persevere through, He is with me. He has never once dropped me, and I don't believe He's going to start now. So my hope for you today, my lovely lady friends, is that you would find joy in your suffering and allow God to build your character so that He might fill your hearts with hope through the Holy Spirit.

Romans 5:3–5—Not only So, but we rejoice in our sufferings because we know that suffering produces perseverance, perseverance, character, and character, hope. And hope does not disappoint us, because God has poured out his love into our hearts by the Holy Spirit whom he has given us.

Dear Heavenly Father, thank You, Lord, for this day even though in the midst of my suffering I sometimes feel despair. I ask, Lord, that You would help me to find the joy. Not the joy that is the same as being happy for my suffering but the joy in knowing that You are with me, and You are building my character and filling me with hope. I pray, Lord, for my sisters today and for all those who call out Your name that in the midst of their suffering they would find You. And as You pour out the Holy Spirit upon us, help us, Lord, to receive. We thank You, Lord, for your grace and mercy today. Amen!

Day 36

May 13

Good morning, my pink sisters. I prayed for you this morning. I read a powerful passage of hope in my devotions this morning in 1 Corinthians 15:51–58. Verse 55 said, "Where, O death, is your victory? Where, O death, is your sting?" Death has no victory over me because of God's grace and the resurrection of Jesus. As I pray for health and ask God to heal me, I am reminded that although I suffer now, one *glorious* day, I will have a new body. As the perishable become imperishable, *glory* be to God! My fears are not in death but in the journey to eternity. I want to live a long happy life, and I would love to feel good all the time and not be sick or ever suffer. This passage reminds me that one day, one *glorious* day, I will live in a body that will never know sickness or decay, pain, fear, or sadness. I cling to that promise today with my body not exactly working the way I would like it to, or feeling 100 percent. I am grateful to God for every breath. Praise God, for His grace and mercy have made me whole. If not in this life, then in the next.

💝 💝 1 Corinthians 55—Where, O death, is your victory? Where, O death, is your sting?

Please read 1 Corinthians 15:51–58. It's awesome!

💝 💝 💝 Dear Heavenly Father, be with me, Lord, as my body aches, and my mind fights off the enemy from his lies. Glory to God, for one day, we shall be imperishable, glory-filled, and whole. No sickness and no pain and with everlasting life. I long for this day, Lord. So from this day until then, may I always feel Your presence and know You are omnipresent. That from this day until then, You have set me on a path. Please, Father, carry me when I feel I cannot take one more step. Remind me of Your promises of eternity. Amen!

Day 37

May 14

 Good morning, my pink sisters. I prayed for you this morning. When I think of how weary I am and how tired my body is, I read Isaiah 40:28–31, and my heart is lifted. "Do you not know? Have you not heard? The Lord is the everlasting God." What hope this brings me. *He* is everlasting. *He* will not grow weary and leave us. In our weary souls, *He* will lift us like eagles, and we will not grow faint. We must have faith that God will not leave us or forsake us. When we are weak, *He* is strong. May we rest in Him today, and in His goodness may we find strength.

Isaiah 40:28–31

Do you not know? Have you not heard? The Lord is the everlasting God, the creator of the ends of the earth. He will not grow tired or weary and his understanding no one can fathom. He gives strength to the weary and increases the power of the weak. Even youths grow tired and weary, and young men stumble and fall; but those who hope in the Lord will renew their strength. They will soar on wings like eagles; they will run and not grow weary, they will walk and not be faint.

💟 💟 💟 Dear Heavenly Father, thank You, Lord. You are so good to us. Lord, we are sometimes weary, and in our human bodies and minds, we cannot refresh ourselves. So we asked today, Lord, that You would lift us on the wings of eagles, that we would run and not grow weary, and that we would continue to walk Your path and not faint. Help our faith, Lord, that we would call upon You, for You are everlasting. Amen!

Day 38

May 17

Good morning, my pink sisters. I prayed for you this morning. Well, this is my last week of radiation. Praise God! Starting next week, I'll be on tamoxifen for five years. One of the things I've been battling is the worry of reoccurrence. Although my doctor has assured me that there's really no chance that it spreads anywhere because of its type of cancer, I worry. Every ache and every pain throws my mind into worry. But my God is an awesome God. And every time my mind goes there, I have to dig deeper into my faith. Once we've gone through something like this, the devil is certainly going to use it to try and keep us weak, but we are not weak. Most of you, women, have endured more than most people can handle. We have walked through the fire with the Lord by our side. So take heart, my sisters. The thoughts and the feelings will come and go, but Jesus is with you always. And we are humans, so we will fear, but the Holy Spirit is within us; and He will always lead you and protect you if you allow Him.

💙 💙 Matthew 6:27—Can anyone of you by worrying add a single hour to your life?

💙 💙 💙 Dear Heavenly Father, be with us today, Lord, as we face the day. Remind us, Lord, that worrying does not add one minute, one hour, or one day to our life. But believing and trusting in You lead us to eternity. May You walk with us today, Lord, in the good and the bad. Allow us to feel Your presence and know we do not walk alone. Amen!

Day 39

May 19

Good morning, my pink sisters. I prayed for you this morning. Well yesterday was a roller coaster of emotions. I opened that emotional door an inch, and Satan stepped right in. I found my mind going to places it had no business being. Things I had turned over to God a long time ago. Why do we take things back once we have turned them over? I ended up telling Satan to pack his lies and get out! I asked God to fill me with the truth, praising Him for what He has done for me and in me. I never thought I would be in a place of freedom in Christ. It was always so hard to turn my mind off, but if we fill our minds and hearts with His praises, there is no room for Satan. Today, when Satan tries to get in your mind, fill yourself with praise and truth then tell him to pack his bag and get out!

Psalm 71:8—My mouth is filled with your praises, declaring your splendor all the day long.

Dear Heavenly Father, please be with us today. In the moments when Satan tries to fill our heads with doubt and worry with things that we have already turned over to you, we ask, Lord, that You would help us to evict him from our minds and our hearts. Help us, Lord, to not even open that door an inch to allow him to get in but to be in constant praise of Your name, declaring your splendor and Your glory throughout our day. Amen!

Day 40

May 21

Good morning, my pink sisters. I prayed for you today. This is it! The last day of radiation, and I'm so happy and relieved it's over. My God is an awesome God, and I give Him *thanks*. I also am grateful that He has brought me to you, ladies. I know your prayers, and love carried me in my times of fear. We have victory through Jesus Christ in all matters that we face. I am sure in my life I will have more trials as God grows me and prepares me for the kingdom. I have learned so much about myself, my God, and my faith through this time. Right now, I will enjoy each day. Tomorrow, I turn fifty-one; next week, I go see my daughter graduate from boot camp and bring her home and then summer. God is good. God is great. Thank you, Lord, for this day.

1 Corinthians 15:57—But thanks be to God! He gives us the victory through our Lord Jesus Christ.

Dear Heavenly Father, I thank You for this day, Lord. You are with us, Lord, in our trials and in our victories. You, Father, are with us when we are lonely and when we are not. I pray, Lord, that today would be a day of victory for many and that You would be with each and every one of us that we would know Your ever-loving presence. Help us, Lord, to be thankful in all circumstances. All glory and honor to You. Amen!

Day 41

May 24

Good morning, my pink sisters, I prayed for you this morning. I am working on being in the right mind-set. Focusing on what God has done for me, and not what Satan is trying to do to me. Our circumstances are not our truth. We will stumble and fall at the enemies' attacks, but God will always be there to lift us. The key is willingness. We are sometimes comfortable in our despair. Please know God is with us—with you. He will pluck you out of the pit and stand you on a solid rock of salvation and righteousness.

Psalm 37:24—That we stumble, he will not fall, for the Lord upholds him with his hand.

Dear Heavenly Father, thank You, God, for Your faithfulness. Even when we stumble, and the enemy moves in, we need to only ask for You, and You are there. Please, Father, continue to uphold us so that we may be found in Your presence, safe from the enemies' attacks. Place us, Lord, on the solid rock. Amen!

Day 42

May 25

Good morning, my pink sisters, I prayed for you this morning. Every morning, I wake up, get my coffee, sit, and read my bible. Sometimes I watch a sermon or read a devotional. I pray and I start my day. As my day goes by, sometimes I can feel myself being less energized in the Lord. I'm tired, in pain, sometimes tired of people and all the negative influence. Well this morning, Ephesians 6 really got me. I know about "the armor of God," but yet I have not prayed it over myself. God not only wants to break every chain, but He also wants to protect me from the captor (Satan); therefore, pink warriors, stand firm. Be ready for battle. We are warriors, we are brave, and we have God on our side.

 Ephesians 6:10–18

Finally, be strong in the Lord and in his mighty power. Put on the full armor of God so that you can take your stand against the devil's schemes. For our struggle is not against flesh and blood, but against the rulers, against the authorities, against the powers of this dark world and against the spiritual forces of evil in the heavenly realms. Therefore put on the full armor of God, so that when the day of evil comes, you may be able to stand your ground and after you have done everything, to stand. Stand firm then, with the belt of truth buckled around your waist, with the breastplate of righteousness in place, and with your feet fitted with the readiness that comes from the gospel of peace. In addition to all this, take up the shield of faith, with which you can extinguish all the flaming arrows of the evil one. Take the helmet of salvation and the sword of the spirit, which is the word of God. And pray in the Spirit on all occasions with all kinds of prayers and requests. With this in mind, be alert and always keep on praying for all the saints.

Dear Heavenly Father, thank You for Your protection, Lord. May we suit up before heading out today. You are for us, Lord, who shall we fear? When we are feeling weak, Lord, and feeling defeated, let us remember that we wear Your armor. We are fully protected from the evil one. No weapon formed against us can stand when we are suited up in Christ. Amen!

Philippians 4:6–7—(6) Do not be anxious about anything, but in every situation, by prayer and petition, with thanksgiving, present your request to God. (7) And the peace of God, which transcends all understanding, will guard your hearts and your minds in Christ Jesus.

About the Author

Debra Ronan is a wife and mother. Debra and her husband, Sean, have been married for thirty-two years. They have three adult children: Joseph, thirty-one; Ryan, twenty-seven; and Irene, twenty-one. Debra (Debbie) resides in Sebastian, Florida. In January 2021, Debra was diagnosed with breast cancer; and through this journey, *In the Morning* was created. Debra wants to share the message that you are not alone, God is with you. Debra's hope is to get this message to all who are alone or who are feeling lonely. Debra would like to thank God for his grace and for always being with her. Debra would like to thank her husband, Sean, and her family for all their love and support and to her Pink sisters for being there every step of the way.

CPSIA information can be obtained
at www.ICGtesting.com
Printed in the USA
LVHW070000301022
731897LV00010B/142

9 781638 858546